BEI GRIN MACHT SICH IHR WISSEN BEZAHLT

- Wir veröffentlichen Ihre Hausarbeit, Bachelor- und Masterarbeit

- Ihr eigenes eBook und Buch - weltweit in allen wichtigen Shops

- Verdienen Sie an jedem Verkauf

Jetzt bei www.GRIN.com hochladen und kostenlos publizieren

Hans-Jürgen Borchardt

Angebote erfolgreich formulieren

Kundenwünsche erkennen und erfüllen

GRIN Verlag

Bibliografische Information der Deutschen Nationalbibliothek:

Die Deutsche Bibliothek verzeichnet diese Publikation in der Deutschen Nationalbibliografie; detaillierte bibliografische Daten sind im Internet über http://dnb.d-nb.de/ abrufbar.

Dieses Werk sowie alle darin enthaltenen einzelnen Beiträge und Abbildungen sind urheberrechtlich geschützt. Jede Verwertung, die nicht ausdrücklich vom Urheberrechtsschutz zugelassen ist, bedarf der vorherigen Zustimmung des Verlages. Das gilt insbesondere für Vervielfältigungen, Bearbeitungen, Übersetzungen, Mikroverfilmungen, Auswertungen durch Datenbanken und für die Einspeicherung und Verarbeitung in elektronische Systeme. Alle Rechte, auch die des auszugsweisen Nachdrucks, der fotomechanischen Wiedergabe (einschließlich Mikrokopie) sowie der Auswertung durch Datenbanken oder ähnliche Einrichtungen, vorbehalten.

Impressum:

Copyright © 2010 GRIN Verlag, Open Publishing GmbH
Druck und Bindung: Books on Demand GmbH, Norderstedt Germany
ISBN: 978-3-640-75830-2

Dieses Buch bei GRIN:

http://www.grin.com/de/e-book/162039/angebote-erfolgreich-formulieren

GRIN - Your knowledge has value

Der GRIN Verlag publiziert seit 1998 wissenschaftliche Arbeiten von Studenten, Hochschullehrern und anderen Akademikern als eBook und gedrucktes Buch. Die Verlagswebsite www.grin.com ist die ideale Plattform zur Veröffentlichung von Hausarbeiten, Abschlussarbeiten, wissenschaftlichen Aufsätzen, Dissertationen und Fachbüchern.

Besuchen Sie uns im Internet:

http://www.grin.com/

http://www.facebook.com/grincom

http://www.twitter.com/grin_com

Angebote erfolgreich formulieren

Mit dem Schreiben von Angeboten ist es wie mit allen anderen Leistungen: Wer sich nicht von den anderen positiv unterscheidet, gewinnt nur, wenn er der Billigste ist.

Mit einem 08/15-Angebot hat man kaum Chancen, einen Auftrag zu gewinnen. Mal abgesehen davon, dass man einen Auftrag auch nicht verdient - ein Angebot von der Stange missachtet schließlich sämtliche Kundenerwartungen.

Aufträge gewinnt nur, wer sich bewusst ist, dass jeder Kunde mit der Vergabe eines Auftrages konkrete Vorstellungen verbindet, die auch erfüllt werden müssen. Und wer sich in die Lage eines Auftraggebers versetzt, weiß, dass die Gewinnung eines Auftrages weit vor der eigentlichen Angebotsabgabe beginnt.

Überlegen Sie selbst: Angenommen, Sie möchten einen Auftrag vergeben, was erwarten Sie? Im Wesentlichen vermutlich diese vier Aspekte:

- dass der Auftrag pünktlich und zuverlässig erledigt wird
- dass die Qualität der Arbeiten exzellent ist und reklamationsfrei ausgeführt wird
- dass gehalten wird, was versprochen wurde und
- dass der Auftragnehmer glaubwürdig ist.

Erfolgversprechend ist ein Angebot also immer dann, wenn

- Sie als potenzieller Auftragnehmer bereits beim Erstkontakt Vertrauen herstellen konnten und
- das schriftliche Angebot immer eine Bestätigung vorab getroffener Zusagen enthält.

Erstes Beispiel: Ein Hausbesitzer will sein Dachgeschoss ausbauen lassen. Dazu lädt er zwei Schreinerfirmen ein. Beide Firmeninhaberbesuchen den Interessenten und machen sich vor Ort ein Bild von den Vorstellungen des Auftraggebers sowie vom zu erwartenden Arbeitsumfang. Nach einigen Tagen treffen die beiden Angebote ein.

Angebot Betrieb A

Ausbau des Dachgeschosses

Sehr geehrte Fam. Meier,

Wir danken Ihnen für die Ihre Anfrage und bieten unsere Leistungen wie folgt an:

Ausbau des Dachgeschosses einschl.
17cm Isolierung. Wandmaterial
Gipskartonplatten, wie besprochen   EURO ….

Lieferung und Verlegung von 44m²
Parkettfußboden, Eiche, wie besprochen

Schleifen des Parkettfußboden incl. Fertiglack	EURO …..
Lieferung und Montage von Rahmen und Tür einschl. Beschlag, wie besprochen	EURO ….
Zzgl. 19% MwSt.	EURO …..
Gesamtpreis	EURO …..

Wir würden uns freuen, wenn Sie uns mit dem Auftrag betrauen würden.

Mit freundlichen Grüßen

Legt man das o. g. Raster mit den vier Aspekten an, die erfüllt sein müssen, damit der Kunde zufrieden ist, ergibt sich für das Beispiel-Angebot ein trauriges Bild:

- Pünktlichkeit und Zuverlässigkeit?
  Von einer zuverlässigen und pünktlichen Abwicklung
  keine Rede.
- Werden die Arbeiten qualitativ mustergültig und reklamationsfrei ausgeführt? Kein einziges Wort zu diesen Erwartungen.
- Wird gehalten, was versprochen wird? Kein Hinweis, nirgends.
- Ist der Auftragnehmer glaubwürdig? Kaum, denn das Angebot ist so allgemein, dass dieser Schreiner viele Möglichkeiten hätte zu manipulieren.

Besser ist es, Andeutungen, Zusagen oder gar Versprechen immer schriftlich zu bestätigen! Hat der Kunde die Zusagen schwarz auf weiß, gewinnen Sie mehrere Vorteile:

- Indem Sie den Kunden über Details informieren, schaffen SieVertrauen und ein gemeinsames Fundament für die weitere Kommunikation.
- Sie wirken vertrauenswürdig und seriöser, weil Sie einerseits kontrollierbar werden, weil Sie Kompetenz und Einfühlungsvermögen demonstrieren und weil erkennbar ist, dass Sie sich die Zeit für ein individuelles Angebot genommen haben.
- Im Normalfall wird der Kunde Ihre offene Kommunikation mit einem Vertrauensvorschuss belohnen. Er erkennt, dass Sie im Gegensatz zur Konkurrenz auf seine (meisten nicht formulierten Erwartungen) eingehen.

Das heißt natürlich nicht, dass Sie mit einem gut geschriebenen Angebot den Auftrag schon in der Tasche haben. Aber Sie verbessern Ihre Chancen beträchtlich, wenn das Angebot etwa wie folgt geschrieben wird:

Angebot Betrieb B

Der Ausbau des Dachgeschosses in Ihrem Haus

Guten Tag Familie Meier,

für das informative Gespräch bei Ihnen bedanke ich mich. Ich bin überzeugt, dass Ihnen der Ausbau des Dachgeschosses, so wie Sie es jetzt geplant haben, viel Freude bereiten wird. Meine Mitarbeiter und ich -das verspreche ich- werden mit größter Sorgfalt arbeiten, damit alles so wird, wie Sie es sich vorstellen. Selbstverständlich werden wir auch die mit dem Ausbau verbundenen Belästigungen so gering wie möglich halten. Ihre Terminwünsche werden wir selbstverständlich genau einhalten.

Aufstellung und Kosten der ausgesuchten Materialien:

1. Dachisolierung, insgesamt 112m²

1.1 Kontrolle der Dachhaut. (Sollte diese undicht sein, kann Wasser eindringen und das Isoliermaterial verliert einen Teil seiner Wirkung)
1.2 Einbringen der hochwärmedämmenden Steinwolle, in einer Stärke von 17cm. Wärmeleitfähigkeit von nur 0,32 W/mK. Damit entspricht die Dämmung des Daches in allen Punkten der neuen EnEV, die seit 2009 gilt.
1.3 Ausbau mit 12mm starken Gipskartonplatten. Abschließend tapezierfertig gespachtelt.

Gesamtpreis für Pos. 1. bis 1.3   EURO …..

2. Fußboden, 44m²
Der Fußboden ist gleichmäßig eben und muss für die Verlegung des Parketts nicht vorbehandelt werden.
2.1 Als Fußboden haben Sie Eiche, Stabparkett ausgesucht.
Farbe: hell
2.2 Die Verlegung erfolgt im Oxford-Verband.
2.3 Nach der Verlegung wird das Parkett 3x geschliffen und anschließend mit speziellem Lack versiegelt.

Gesamtpreis für Pos. 2. bis 2.3   EURO …..

3. Holztür mit Rahmen
Die Holztür mit Glasausschnitt, Furnier Eiche, hell, und die Beschläge haben Sie aus dem Katalog ausgewählt.
3.1 Passgenauer Einbau von Rahmen und Tür   EURO …..

Zzgl. 19% MwSt.   EURO …..

Gesamtpreis   EURO …..

Ich werde Sie am Donnerstag anrufen und mich erkundigen, ob Sie noch Fragen haben. Möchten Sie einen Eindruck gewinnen, wie wir arbeiten und welche Qualität wir liefern, geben wir Ihnen gerne mehrere Referenzadressen begeisterter Kunden.

Sollten Sie noch irgendwelche Veränderungen wünschen, ist das kein Problem. Wir sind flexibel. Das gilt auch für die Zusammenarbeit mit der Elektrofirma, die mit der Verlegung der Leitungen beauftragt werden muss.

Wenn Sie alles aus einer Hand haben wollen, übernehmen wir, bzw. ein zertifizierter Meisterbetrieb diese Arbeit. Wenn Sie selbst eine Elektrofirma beauftragen, bitten wir um den Namen bzw. den Ansprechpartner, damit wir unsere Arbeiten „nahtlos verbinden und ausführen können. Danke.

Viele Grüße von XYZ,
das Team mit den zufriedenen Kunden!

Fazit
Angebot ist nicht gleich Angebot. Erfolgversprechende Angebote enthalten zwei Aspekte: Zum einen müssen darin die Erwartungen des Kunden widergespiegelt und bestätigt werden. Und zum anderen sollten Angebote eine individuelle Ansprache führen. Denn nur Kunden, die sich ernst genommen und gut aufgehoben fühlen, erteilen auch Aufträge. Das Beispiel zeigt, dass sich - unabhängig von der Branche und Unternehmensgröße - Angebote stets individualisieren lassen und damit aus der Masse hervorstechen.

Außerdem sind auch in individualisierten Angebote Textpassagen, die sich immer wiederholen. Also, wenn einmal ein Muster erstellt ist, hat man für alle anderen eine Grundvorlage.

Hans-Jürgen Borchardt
November 2010

YOUR KNOWLEDGE HAS VALUE

- We will publish your bachelor's and master's thesis, essays and papers

- Your own eBook and book -
  sold worldwide in all relevant shops

- Earn money with each sale

Upload your text at www.GRIN.com
and publish for free

Martina Olonschek, Klaus Köhring

Recension of Arthur Millers "Death of a Salesman"

Bibliographic information published by the German National Library:

The German National Library lists this publication in the National Bibliography; detailed bibliographic data are available on the Internet at http://dnb.dnb.de .

This book is copyright material and must not be copied, reproduced, transferred, distributed, leased, licensed or publicly performed or used in any way except as specifically permitted in writing by the publishers, as allowed under the terms and conditions under which it was purchased or as strictly permitted by applicable copyright law. Any unauthorized distribution or use of this text may be a direct infringement of the author s and publisher s rights and those responsible may be liable in law accordingly.

Imprint:

Copyright © 2006 GRIN Verlag, Open Publishing GmbH
Print and binding: Books on Demand GmbH, Norderstedt Germany
ISBN: 978-3-656-87806-3

This book at GRIN:

http://www.grin.com/en/e-book/76185/recension-of-arthur-millers-death-of-a-salesman

GRIN - Your knowledge has value

Since its foundation in 1998, GRIN has specialized in publishing academic texts by students, college teachers and other academics as e-book and printed book. The website www.grin.com is an ideal platform for presenting term papers, final papers, scientific essays, dissertations and specialist books.

Visit us on the internet:

http://www.grin.com/

http://www.facebook.com/grincom

http://www.twitter.com/grin_com

Recension

Arthur Miller
„Death of a Salesman"

processed passage of text

Penguin books:
page 25 (Willy: "Bernard is not well liked is he?") – page 27
(Willy: "What do we owe?")

Martina Olonschek

Klaus Köhring

Table of Contents

Table of Contents 2

1. Analysis of the passage in the text (Penguin: page 25, "Willy: Bernard is not well liked, is he?" – page 27, "Willy: "What do we owe?") 3

   1.1. Characterization of Willy Loman 3

   1.2. Willy' relationship to Linda 4

   1.3. Relationship between a father and his sons 5

   1.3.1. Biff, the star 5

   1.3.2. Happy, the spectator 6

   1.4. Dialogue or monologue? 6

2. Relation between the passage and the drama "Death of a Salesman" 8

   2.1. Charley – Antagonist or best friend? 9

   2.2. Destroyed dreams 10

   2.3. The final payment 12

3. Evaluation – Marxist literary criticism 14

4. Sources 15

   Literature 15

   Internet-sources 15

1. Analysis of the passage in the text (Penguin: page 25, "Willy: Bernard is not well liked, is he?" – page 27, "Willy: "What do we owe?")

This passage from the first act of Arthur Miller's drama "Death of a Salesman" displays one of the numerous flashbacks of Willy Loman, who represents the main character and moreover a complex round character. With this reflection of the past the reader or spectator is able to share in Willy's and his former family life; a family life that is harmonious, easy, joyful or simply all in all perfect.

1.1. Characterization of Willy Loman

For Willy this ideal world is very important as ideals are in general. He places special value on a good image, which can be seen in the very first question of the passage *"Bernard is not well liked, is he?"*[1], which he addresses to his sons Biff and Happy. With the simile *"you're both built like Adonoises"*[1], which Willy is thankful for and moreover very proud of, and the statement that his sons *"are going to be five times ahead of [Bernard]"*[1] because of their appearance, it becomes clear that he is of the opinion that attractiveness which results in *"personal interest"*[1] and popularity is the only way to become big in business – which is pretty unrealistic already because good grades are necessary to enrol in college, and contents taught in college are in the majority of cases necessary to become big in business. It is furthermore visible that Willy builds his hopes on Biff and Happy. For them he is a role model and he seems really confident of being a good one: *"Be liked and you will never want. You take me, for instance. I never have to wait in line [...]."*[2] He is also sure of the fact that he is well known and welcome everywhere he goes which is indicated by the following statement *"'Willy Loman is here!' That's all they have to know [...]."*[3] Another pleasure in Willy's life is to share his work with his sons by telling them stories about it. He then tends to exaggerate, as it is seen in his self praise-hyperbole *"knocked 'em cold in Providence, slaughtered 'em in Boston."*[3], in order to bring his business success near to them.

---

[1] Miller, Arthur (1961):„Death of a Salesman". London, page 25
[2] Miller, Arthur (1961):„Death of a Salesman". London, page 25f
[3] Miller, Arthur (1961):„Death of a Salesman". London, page 26

1.2. Willy' relationship to Linda

Willy and his wife's Linda's marriage seems very loving and harmonious as they address each other with really tender nicknames like *"dear"*[3] and *"sweatheart"*[3]. Their relationship is based on a traditional distribution of roles and it becomes obvious that Willy is the head of the family when he corrects Linda *"Chevrolet, Linda [...]"*[3] after she asks him about the *"Chevvy"*[4]. This traditional relationship is furthermore perceptible in his old style politeness because he does not want his wife to heft. This moreover indicates that children have to respect their parents which Willy clarifies with the rhetorical question *"since when do you let your mother carry wash up the stairs?"*[4]. But beside traditions their relationship is based on lies. When asked about his earnings Willy absolutely exaggerates his profit (*"[...] I was selling thousands and thousands [...]"*[4] or *"I did five hundred gross in Providence and seven hundred gross in Boston"*[5]) and does not straighten it out before Linda gets too exited about the fact that his commission would clear all their debts. He then starts stumbling and confesses that not his commission but his profit amounts 200 dollars, which is probably still not the whole truth and only an attempt to not disappoint Linda (*"Well – I did – about a hundred and eighty gross in Providence . Well, no – it came to – roughly two hundred gross on the whole trip."*[5]).

Now the traditional distribution of roles changes. Willy is now in the position where he feels to be accountable to Linda. So the 'slaughterer of Boston', who is admired by everyone, is actually degraded to meat stock, the weakest link. He tries to get out of this misery by blaming others for his belying performance when he excuses himself with the statement that *"[...] three of the stores where half-closed for inventory in Boston"*[5]. He then wants to distract from the bad news and presents himself in the proper light again by mentioning that he *"otherwise [...] woulda broke records"*[5].

Linda is in the position of the bookkeeper. There could be several reasons for this. Maybe Willy is not able to do this job or she wants to control him. She is interested in Willy's work and his profit and asks questions which inconvenience him. Now she is

---

[4] Miller, Arthur (1961):„Death of a Salesman". London, page 26
[5] Miller, Arthur (1961):„Death of a Salesman". London, page 27

the boss, but a really nice one, because she is still his loving wife. She is able to cover her frustration and still finds words to build him up (*"Well, it makes seventy dollars and some pennies. That's very good."*[5]) when he has failed. The fact that she even mentions the pennies elucidates her optimism. Probably, she is already used to his overstatements and therefore not very surprised when he eventually corrects them. An indicator for this can be found in the secondary text, the stage direction that she answers his confession *"without hesitation"*[5]. Both, Willy and Linda are concerned about their debts. Their whole conversation about his profit concludes in Willy's question *"what do we owe?"*[5]. He is therefore more pessimistic than his wife and highlights the serious reality again.

1.3. Relationship between a father and his sons

Both, Biff and Happy really admire their dad. For them, and especially for Biff, he is the most important person. This is indicated by Biff's statement *"ah, when Pop comes home [my friends] can wait"*[6]. They have great respect for Willy and would never contradict him when receiving orders like carrying the laundry (*"Grab hold there, boy"*[6], *"Where to, mom?"*[6]). They believe like their father in the traditional old style politeness, which is not surprising as their were raised by Willy.

1.3.1. Biff, the star

Willy and Linda are very proud of their eldest son Biff which becomes visible with utterances like *"The way they obey him!"*[6] and *"Oh, the whole block'll be at that [football] game"*[7]. He is very popular and therefore Willy's ideal of a perfect son and student. Willy does not care about Biff's grades in school but is more impressed and interested in his outward appearance and his athletic skills as a football player. Biff is aware of being special which is a result of the overwhelming attention and love he receives from his parents and especially Willy wherefore he is maybe a little too self-confident. He treats his friends as his subject when he says *"I think I'll have them sweep out the furnace room"*[6] and even gives them orders like with the polysyndeton *"George and Sam and Frank, come out back! We're hangin' up the wash!"*[6]. He does not know better, because he gets positive feedback from both Linda and Willy. They support these

---

[6] Miller, Arthur (1961):„Death of a Salesman". London, page 26
[7] Miller, Arthur (1961):„Death of a Salesman". London, page 27

acts and Biff's feeling to be in a higher position than his fellows with instigations like "*[...] you better go down to your friends [...]. They don't know what to do with themselves*"[6] and "*you better go down and tell them what do do*"[6]. Surprising is the fact that Biff's friends do follow his demands ("*All right! Okay, Biff.*"[6]).

1.3.2. Happy, the spectator

Happy, however, does not anywhere near obtain as much attention as his older brother. It seems that he lacks self-confidence because he does not speak very much and when he does he only repeats Biff's utterances or agrees with him ("*That's right*"[8]). His attempts to attract notice ("*I'm losing weight, you notice, Pop?*"[6]) and jumping at him (stage direction: "*On his back*"[6]) fail by being ignored. Neither Willy nor Linda lose a word about their younger son, they do not show any interest, which probably confirms Biff's believe in being someone special even more.

1.4. Dialogue or monologue?

Based on the fact that this scene happens in Willy's imagination the actual place of action sets in the Loman's kitchen with Willy sitting at the kitchen table having a glass of milk (*information is given on the earlier page 21*). He is alone - although Willy is of another opinion, though - and therefore his dialogues to his imaginary wife and sons are strictly speaking a monologue and even a soliloquy because no other person is present in reality. The difference to monologues in other dramas is that this monologue is not accepted as normal by the reader or spectator. This one is comparable with a monologue which can be watched on an open street, for example. Just like these mumbling persons Willy is considered to be 'crazy' or 'retarded'.

Because only the reader or spectator knows what is going on in Willy's memory and because he can see and hear Willy and his dialog partners, what his real sons and wife are not able to, this flashback is dramatic irony. The external communication like the stage directions and the younger characters that are invisible to the real characters give more information to the reader/spectator than the internal communication, the speech between the real characters, could do.

---

[8] Miller, Arthur (1961):„Death of a Salesman". London, page 25

The reader/spectator understands the context of the conversation between Willy and his imaginary family - and this is the actual reason why this imaginary family does exist - whereas the real family only gets to hear Willy's - to them - confusing statements.

There is no actual evidence given in the secondary text, but since the boys play football, wherefore space is necessary, I consider that Willy's imagination is located in the garden. Through the whole passage of the text this does not change.

2. Relation between the passage and the drama "Death of a Salesman"

The analysed excerpt from the drama "Death of a Salesman" (compare with 1. – 1.4.) is a really good example to show one of Willy Loman's many getaways from reality. They indicate that he very clings to the past. In his case this is not surprising as his life is not exactly successful and satisfying. The setting that is described at the beginning of the first act is an indicator for this and gives a detailed imagination of Willy's seedy feeling: The Loman's *"small, fragile-seeming home"*[9] is furnished absolutely spartan and surrounded on all sides by other apartment houses[10], which indicates the Loman's poverty and furthermore that Willy feels cornered. The high walls of the other houses block the sunlight which makes it impossible for Willy to grow anything in his garden *("[…] you can't raise a carrot in the backyard."*[11]). This is depressing for him because it prevents him to leave anything behind that would remind of him when he is gone some day (*"I don't have a thing in the ground."*[12]).

The only fitment in the house that seems glamorous is the *"silver athletic trophy"*[13] on a shelf over Willy and Linda's bed. Since being close to Willy in his sleep – and therefore maybe a protector – and being the only non-implement in the house this trophy is probably Willy's greatest treasure. It reminds him of the good old times when everything in his life went fine, when he and his sons, and especially Biff, used to be successful and well liked. Success and a grandiose image are for Willy the most important and maybe the only goals to be achieved in a man's life (*"I got a good job"*[14], *"be liked and you will never want"*[15]). But he not only has these dreams, he even pretends that these dreams have actually come true and he does not accept any deviations of this illusion as it gets visible with his statement *"I won't have you mending stockings in this house!"*[16]. Saying this it becomes clear that he does not want anyone to see that he cannot even afford new stockings for his wife. (*Another interpretation can be found in 2.2.*)

---

[9] Miller, Arthur (1961):„Death of a Salesman". London, page 7
[10] compare with Miller, Arthur (1961):„Death of a Salesman". London, page 7
[11] Miller, Arthur (1961):„Death of a Salesman". London, page 12
[12] Miller, Arthur (1961):„Death of a Salesman". London, page 96
[13] Miller, Arthur (1961):„Death of a Salesman". London, page 7
[14] Miller, Arthur (1961):„Death of a Salesman". London, page 34
[15] Miller, Arthur (1961):„Death of a Salesman". London, page 25f
[16] Miller, Arthur (1961):„Death of a Salesman". London, page 31

When wallowing in his memories the setting changes which is described in the stage directions in the first act. Then there are no boundaries like walls or doors[17] which is an indicator that Willy is absolutely carefree and satisfied. Here Willy is in the position to make fun of others or even to abuse them (*"Don't be a pest, Bernard! […] What an anaemic!"*[18], *"[the Lomans laugh]"*[18]); here he is the father of a grandiose and popular football player with a promising looking career (*"They'll be calling [Biff] another Red Grange. Twenty-five thousand a year."*[19]); here he gets in contact with a successful family member, his brother Ben (*"[…] When I walked out of [the jungle] I was […] rich!"*[20]); and here he does not have to care about his old neighbour Charley's good advices.

2.1. Charley – Antagonist or best friend?

Charley is a large, laconic and immovable man[21] but compared to Willy he is successful in his job and seems satisfied with his life and himself. The statement *"There's some money – fifty dollars."*[22] indicates that he does not have to care or lie about money, no, he is even in the position to lend Willy enough money so that he can pretend at home to still getting his salary. On the one hand Willy is thankful for receiving this 'donation', because he keeps out of embarrassing trouble, but on the other hand he is jealous of Charley's career which he was never able to achieve. It is hard for Willy to understand how Charley has become so big even though he is not well liked. But it shocks him even more when he realizes that Charley's son Bernard, the nerd who he used to make fun of, *"[argues] a case in front of the Supreme Court"*[23] and is therefore in the highest position an American lawyer can be. Bernard reached something that Biff did not (*"What – what's the secret?" "How – how did you? Why didn't [Biff] ever catch on?"*[24]). With Willy's statement *"the Supreme Court! And he didn't even mention it!"*[23] it is noticeable that Willy can barely believe Bernard's modesty, that he does not tell the whole world about his success as Willy would do – if he could. This clarifies a very

---

[17] compare with Miller, Arthur (1961):„Death of a Salesman". London, page 7
[18] Miller, Arthur (1961):„Death of a Salesman". London, page 25
[19] Miller, Arthur (1961):„Death of a Salesman". London, page 70
[20] Miller, Arthur (1961):„Death of a Salesman". London, page 40f
[21] compare with Miller, Arthur (1961):„Death of a Salesman". London, page 34
[22] Miller, Arthur (1961):„Death of a Salesman". London, page 75
[23] Miller, Arthur (1961):„Death of a Salesman". London, page 75
[24] Miller, Arthur (1961):„Death of a Salesman". London, page 72

important difference between Willy and Charley and moreover between Biff and Bernard. The Lomans only pretend to be something they are not whereas their 'opponents' manage their life without mentioning a word about it ("*He don't have to [mention it] – he's gonna do it*"[23]). To them image is not as important, they know that they cannot and will never be able to feed their family with only a good reputation. To put it briefly - they live in reality.

Charley knows about Willy's job situation and tiredness. He knows that Willy only gets his commission but no regular salary. He knows that Willy is embarrassed because of this and he also knows that Willy tries to hide his misery from Linda. In order to help he offers Willy more than once a fair job in his office which would be a sudden exit out of all these problems ("*You want a job?*"[25], "*[…] You can make fifty dollars a week. And I won't send you on the road.*"[26]) but Willy is to proud to take it, to proud to admit that he needs help, to proud to accept any help from a nerd ("*I don't want your goddam job!*"[26], "*I can't work for you […].*"[27]). Charley is an enormous patient person since he copes with Willy's changes of mood ("*You big ignoramus!*"[26] and then "*Charley, I'm strapped […] I don't know what to do.*"[26]) and because he offers his help and friendship over and over again although Willy only finds words to insult and offend him. It is only when Willy has collected the money for the last payment of his insurance that he is able to tell Charley how he really feels. He probably finally shows weakness because he has nothing to lose anymore. The words "*Charley, you're the only friend I got. Isn't that remarkable*"[28] are Willy's last ones addressing Charley before he commits suicide.

2.2. Destroyed dreams

If compared with 1., 1.3. and 1.3.1. it becomes obvious that Willy and Biff really respect and love each other. They just simply have the perfect father-son relationship. Biff trusts his father and is of the opinion – like Willy himself – that Willy has huge influence over others ("*because if he saw the kind of man you are […] I'm sure he'd come

---

[25] Miller, Arthur (1961):„Death of a Salesman". London, page 33
[26] Miller, Arthur (1961):„Death of a Salesman". London, page 76
[27] Miller, Arthur (1961):„Death of a Salesman". London, page 77
[28] Miller, Arthur (1961):„Death of a Salesman". London, page 77

through for me."[29]) and that nothing and nobody could stop him and his plans. He is therefore confident that his successful father can talk him out of any trouble.

Biff believes in this illusion until he catches his perfect loving father with another woman in a hotel room in Boston. He is absolutely shocked and disappointed and realizes for the first time that his father is not this trustworthy loving and respectful man but a cheater and liar. Suddenly he loses all his trust in Willy (*"[the teacher] wouldn't listen to you*"[30]) and furthermore he loses his self-assurance which is indicated with Bernard's statement that *"he came back after that month [in Boston] and took his sneakers [...] down in the cellar, and burned them up in the furnace*"[31]. His belief in the American dream that he will be big sometime, popular and rich, that he can reach any goal he has is destroyed all of a sudden because he cannot believe in something a cheater and liar has taught him. There are no goals left in his life so that he has problems to gain foothold in professional life.

But it is not only Biff who suffers from the meeting in the hotel. Watching how Biff throws away his talent and career Willy's expectations to be the proud father of a famous football star begin to lack whereas his frustration and his guilty conscious towards Biff and Linda grow. Every time he sees her mending stockings it reminds him of his extramarital affair because he always gave the woman - instead of Linda - a pack of new stockings. This affair changed his perfect family life dramatically and he therefore gets always very angry when being confronted with his mistake (*"I won't have you mending stockings in this house!*"[32]). Instead of confiding to Linda he prefers to live with this lie that obviously bears him down in order to re-establish the lost but so important perfect family life. Biff, however, apprehends with the years that a life cannot be based on lies or wrong ideals. He had to experience that a good image and an arrogant self-confidence is not – as he always had been taught – superior than an order-giving position. Compared to Willy he has eventually found the exit from a world of illusions to the real world and moreover the chance to become happy.

---

[29] Miller, Arthur (1961):„Death of a Salesman". London, page 93
[30] Miller, Arthur (1961):„Death of a Salesman". London, page 95
[31] Miller, Arthur (1961):„Death of a Salesman". London, page 74
[32] Miller, Arthur (1961):„Death of a Salesman". London, page 31

2.3. The final payment

Willy Loman has lost his friendship to his son Biff, he has been fired by a man whose father he could be ("*Your father [...] asked me what I thought of the name Howard [...]*"[33]) and he has lost his position as the head of the family. Linda loves and respects him as she always did but she has taken over the role of a babysitter. She really cares for her husband and always has an eye on him. She actually even controls Willy as she already did when Willy was younger ("*Did you sell anything?*"[34]) but does it more energetically now that Willy got old and confused ("*You got your glasses?*"[35], "*And a handkerchief?*"[35], "*And your saccharine?*"[35]).

Willy is aware of the fact that he has become weaker ("*I'm tired to the death.*"[36]) that he even undersells himself when talking to Howard, his boss ("*If I could take home – well, sixty-five dollars a week [...]*"[37], then "*all I need [...] is fifty dollars a week*"[37], then "*if I had forty dollars a week*"[38] and finally "*Howard, you've got to let me go to Boston [without any payment]!*"[39] only to keep his beloved job as a salesman, his image. When this fails Willy's end has come. He gives up his life but still not his dream of being big. Inspired by his imaged brother Ben, who appears in a lot of Willy's flashbacks but also every once in a while in Willy's present imagination, he is looking forward to finding happiness and luck and wealth. Ben attracts Willy with hopeful metaphorical promises like "*It's dark there, but full of diamonds*"[40] and "*a perfect proposition all around*"[40] to come with him and follow him to the redemptive and bright death. Furthermore winged to commit suicide is Willy by the thought of Biff being finally able to succeed with the twenty thousand dollars from Willy's insurance payout. Again it is Ben who gives Willy the idea that his family is better off without him when saying "*Yes, [that boy is going to be] outstanding, with twenty thousand behind him*"[41].

---

[33] Miller, Arthur (1961):„Death of a Salesman". London, page 62
[34] Miller, Arthur (1961):„Death of a Salesman". London, page 27
[35] Miller, Arthur (1961):„Death of a Salesman". London, page 58
[36] Miller, Arthur (1961):„Death of a Salesman". London, page 8
[37] Miller, Arthur (1961):„Death of a Salesman". London, page 62
[38] Miller, Arthur (1961):„Death of a Salesman". London, page 64
[39] Miller, Arthur (1961):„Death of a Salesman". London, page 66
[40] Miller, Arthur (1961):„Death of a Salesman". London, page 107
[41] Miller, Arthur (1961):„Death of a Salesman". London, page 106

Therefore Ben talks Willy into committing suicide, but since Ben only exists in Willy's imagination Willy uses Ben as his conversational partner to find reasons and moreover a supporter of these reason to end his life.

Willy has come to the decision of ending his life a long time before he actually does the last step. He also makes no secret of it and even tells everybody indirectly about his plans. Charley realizes when Willy asks him to "*apologize to Bernard for [him] when [he sees] him*"[42], because Willy could do this himself if he would plan to live on. Stanley, the waiter knows when Willy gives him all of his little money as a tip with the words "*no take it [...]*"[43] and "*[...] I don't need it anymore*"[43] and Linda has to face it when she looks in his desperate eyes. He eventually leaves his beloved family when he knows that they can be absolutely free of worries and debts. On the day of his funeral – a funeral that happens in the family circle instead of being a huge Willy-celebration, as he always wished it to be ("*when [David Singleman] died, hundreds of salesman and buyers were at his funeral*"[44], "*That funeral will be massive*"[45]) – no open payments are left ("*Willy, I made the last payment today*"[46]). For Willy this was the only way to become a hero, the only way out of his and his family's misery and the only way to die with a good image.

In the sense of a drama, Willy is not a tragic hero since he did not die because of an erroneous bad punishment and he is neither of high status nor a really positive character. He chose to die, it was his own decision but the reader/spectator still experiences pity and identifies with Willy and is moreover able to reproduce Willy's reasons to choose the way he does and therefore Willy is despite all the cons a tragic hero.

---

[42] Miller, Arthur (1961):„Death of a Salesman". London, page 77
[43] Miller, Arthur (1961):„Death of a Salesman". London, page 96
[44] Miller, Arthur (1961):„Death of a Salesman". London, page 63
[45] Miller, Arthur (1961):„Death of a Salesman". London, page 100
[46] Miller, Arthur (1961):„Death of a Salesman". London, page 112

3. Evaluation – Marxist literary criticism

The Marxist literary criticism is in my eyes the most suitable approach to explain Arthur Miller's "Death of a Salesman" because here it is a lower economic group that enjoys attention. Willy Loman and his family belong to the base, which is the lower part of the social political context. Willy's goal is to climb to a position of power, the superstructure. The Marxist slogan *"life determines consciousness"*[47] means in Willy's case that his consciousness suffers from his life. Willy is not successful and therefore he is unsatisfied but he does not want to acknowledge to himself that it is the way it is. This is why he escapes into a dream world and as a conclusion consciousness does not really exist. He is not conscious of his miserable life, he believes to be well liked and to be the father of two well liked and successful sons. Willy's ideology is a *"falsifying collectively held system of ideas and beliefs that interpret the world"*[48] namely if someone is *"liked [...] [he] will never want"*[49] and that a nice outward appearance and a wonderful image are the most important characteristics to rule business or even the world.

Another reason why I chose this approach is because of Arthur Miller's relation to Communism. It is not proved that he was a communist himself, but that he knew people that were of this political orientation. The drama was published during the economic post-war boom[50]. This boom was connected with wealth but also a change in the economical life. Like Karl Marx Arthur Miller related *"the historical development of society to that of economics and politics"*[51] in his drama "Death of a Salesman" wherewith his main character Willy Loman is not able to cope with. Willy dreams of wealth but cannot comprehend that times have changed, that a good image does not push anybody into a high position anymore, that it is mainly performance that counts. And it is this attitude that actually ruins him.

---

[47] Meyer, Michael (2005): „English and American Literatures", second edition. Tübingen, page 144
[48] Meyer, Michael (2005): „English and American Literatures", second edition. Tübingen, page 144
[49] Miller, Arthur (1961):„Death of a Salesman". London, page 25 f
[50] compare with http://www.kirjasto.sci.fi/amiller.htm (2003), August 11th 2006, 02:36 am
[51] Meyer, Michael (2005): „English and American Literatures", second edition. Tübingen, page 145

4. Sources

Literature

1) Miller, Arthur (1961):,,Death of a Salesman". London, published by Penguin Books.

2) Meyer, Michael (2005): ,,English and American Literatures", second edition. Tübingen, published by UTB Basics – Narr Francke Attempto.

Internet-sources

3) http://www.kirjasto.sci.fi/amiller.htm (2003), August 11th 2006, 02:36 am